Rooms in the House of Stone

Also by Michael Dorris

The Broken Cord

The Crown of Columbus
(with Louise Erdrich)

A Guide to Research on North American Indians
(with Arlene Hirschfelder and Mary Lou Byler)

Morning Girl

Native Americans 500 Years After
(photographs by Joseph Farber)

Route 2
(with Louise Erdrich)

Working Men

A Yellow Raft in Blue Water

For David

Michael Dorris

Rooms in the
House of Stone

Best wishes

Milkweed Editions

Michael Dorris

3·21·97

Milkweed Editions, 430 First Avenue North, Suite 400, Minneapolis, MN 55401.

Printed in the United States of America
Published in 1993 by Milkweed Editions

Book design by R. W. Scholes
The text of this book was typeset in 11 pt. Joanna by Stanton Publications. It was
printed on acid-free Glatfelter Natural paper by Edwards Brothers.

98 97 96 95 94 93   6 5 4 3 2 1

Publication of Milkweed books is made possible by grant support from the Literature
Program of the National Endowment for the Arts; Dayton Hudson Foundation for
Dayton's and Target Stores; First Bank System Foundation; General Mills Foundation;
Honeywell Foundation; Jerome Foundation; The McKnight Foundation; Andrew W.
Mellon Foundation; Minnesota State Arts Board through an appropriation by the
Minnesota State Legislature; Northwest Area Foundation; I. A. O'Shaughnessy
Foundation; John A. Rollwagen Fund; Star Tribune/Cowles Media Foundation;
Surdna Foundation; James R. Thorpe Foundation; Lila Wallace-Reader's Digest
Literary Publishers Marketing Development Program; and generous individuals.

Library of Congress Cataloging-in-Publication Data

Dorris, Michael.
    Rooms in the house of stone / by Michael Dorris.
        p.   cm. — (Thistle series)
    ISBN 0-915943-70-0
    1. Refugees—Zimbabwe.   2. Food relief—Zimbabwe.   I. Title
II. Series.
HV640.4.Z55D67   1993
362.87'096891—dc20
                                                                    93-16147
                                                                        CIP

Acknowledgments

These pages would not have been possible without the expert guidance and enduring patience of Gerry and Mai Salole, Chris Eldridge, Mark Nyahada, Sipho Ndovlu, Alice Burnette, Peg Blackburn, Phyllis Dobyns, Barnette Baron, Marjorie Benton, Gibson Lampha, Sandi Campbell, Katy Roberts, Mitch Levitas, David Shipley, Bob Berger, Ben Weiser, Doug Foster, and Emilie Buchwald.

Portions of this book have appeared in altered forms in the *New York Times*, *Washington Post*, *Los Angeles Times*, and *Mother Jones* magazine.

For Persia, whose heart is the inspiration
For Pallas, whose energy is the drive
For *Aza*, whose confidence is the hope
and
For Louise, as in all else, the source and the shine

Rooms in the House of Stone

❖

In the summer of 1992, as a new board member of the Save the Children Foundation, I went to Zimbabwe, the House of Stone, and met a child named Disaster. She was born the previous September, a daughter of the Tonga tribe, and now—and until she reaches her fifth birthday or dies—she is eligible, through an emergency Save the Children/Zimbabwe government supplementary feeding program, to receive one meal of corn mush (mealie meal) a day. Even so, she hasn't gained any weight since April.

Disaster is all eyes, alert to every change in her surroundings. She's wrapped in cloth that once was brightly patterned but now is faded, worn thin. Her weight is supported by her mother's hip, cocked at an angle to afford the widest resting place. She is calm, watching, an intelligent consciousness without vocabulary, a vivid presence in the dusty crowd of mothers and seventy infants quietly assembled at the door of the thatch-roof open-air kitchen. I have the feeling that they have long since said everything to each other there is to say, and now they're on hold, caught in a routine, anxious for any variation to be remarkable.

Sometimes when she's able, Disaster's mother, Angeline, who cares for four other children—two of whose parents are dead from AIDS—supplements the starchy charity diet with a wild fruit she knows how to find in the bush. Before serving, she cooks it, peels it, cooks it again with ashes to neutralize its natural poison. Twice she's located a large root she digs out of the cement earth and serves raw.

"Does it taste good?" I ask the interpreter to inquire in the way of ordinary conversation.

Angeline is a woman a good twenty years my junior, dressed in a chartreuse Malibu Surf T-shirt, a colorful item from the bin of donated clothing distributed earlier in the month. She's perfectly willing to suffer a visitor's questions, for they break the monotony of a day whose highlight is her daughter's single serving of food, but now she looks at me politely as though we have experienced a language problem. She nudges the translator to be more precise.

"It's food," she repeats distinctly in Tonga, correcting what she takes to be my poor comprehension.

❖

Most adult Zimbabweans, unlike their counterparts in Ethiopia, Sudan, or Somalia, have never before had to worry about basic sustenance. Their thirteen-year-old nation is normally an exporter of grain, a supplier to other parts of Africa, and in and around the capital, the aquifer-fed sprinklers still keep lawns green. Prosperous Harare looks like the rest of Zimbabwe before the rains stopped coming, before this year's agricultural crop failed, before the riverbeds turned to caked mud. For those who still manage to live as they used to, depleting in the process the finite underground resources, the imminent prospect of famine seems the stuff of someone else's very bad dream.

Yet, by most estimates, southern Africa has an immediate and desperate need to import five times the tonnage of food that the nations of the Horn required during the worst hungry years of the 1980s. And hunger is immeasurably worsened by thirst. Caught in severe drought, a population can't walk in search for sustenance. Without water, there is no time to look.

When Disaster—whose name was chosen not for its meaning, but because of its exotic euphony—grows up a bit, she'll spend most of her time walking the ten kilometers to the shallow well dug near the river, where she'll compete with impala and elephant for access to water. She'll try to catch twenty liters, lug it home and return again to the clogged hole—hoping not to meet a starving lion like the one that killed a boy last week, and trusting, because she has no choice, that the silty, loamy soil will act as an effective filter against typhoid bacteria.

If she takes after her mother, Disaster will be beautiful, smiling, shy and strong. She'll own one dress at a time, possess no shoes and live on the edge of survival. She'll defer to males and foreigners and live in a society of women; the men are mostly off working for commercial fishing companies or in the mines. Her ancestral homeland was flooded to make a dam for the hydroelectric power needed in the cities, and now she dwells in a thin-soiled, arid lower veldt, a place where the January summer temperature can reach 120°F, where, in winter, the skies fill with the smoke of slash-and-burn fires.

✤

Here are two facts that should not both be true:

   ◆ There is sufficient food produced every year to feed every human being on the planet.

   ◆ Nearly 800 million people literally go hungry every day, with more than a third of the earth's population—2 billion men and women—malnourished one way or another, according to the United Nations Food and Agriculture Organization.

When our stomachs are full and we are free to think of other matters, we take food for granted; when they're empty, we know only its absence. The tenuous causeway between the two poles is imagination, for empathy and sympathy can clearly coexist as unlinked emotions, separate impulses. Tragedy at a distance, whether measured in time or in mileage, may soften the heart, but it also often discourages action. The farther away a problem is perceived to be, the more likely it will disappear into a cloudy panorama, nameless hills and valleys, backdrop to our foreground, a faint alarm that's hard to heed above the din of local chimes. Our ears buffered, we overhear another's peril as muted noise emanating through the closed door to a little used room, a room inhabited by people who aren't addressing us and whose cries, when they come, demand no more involvement from us than perhaps our duty to dial 911 and alert someone in charge.

And yet each of us, at one time or another, in one way or

[15]

another, has assumed responsibility for the welfare of a child, a parent, a spouse, a friend. Each of us has experienced physical dependency when we were young or ill or down on our luck. Each of us has occasionally visited joy and grief, contentment and disappointment, gain and loss. We have no excuse not to recognize the echoes.

At what point, at which of the concentric circles of diminishing impact that surrounds us, does the magnetism of our immediate concern disappear? If moral obligation begins with a categorical imperative for self-preservation, how broadly do we describe our province? If charity begins at home, where does the property line end?

There's no natural closure to need in this world, yet our capacity for emotional or financial reaction is not without limit. Our sense of theoretical justice is constantly assailed by paradox: it's not fair that resources are so inequitably distributed, not right that we have so much when others have nothing. But, we argue in our own defense, we work hard for our money. It doesn't fall from the sky. If we ask for help, we keep scrupulous account, pay back with interest. We earn our good fortune. If everyone in the world were simply as industrious and wise as we, there would be no chronic need for handouts, no undentable poverty.

These rationalizations, however often or loudly proclaimed, turn out to be more fragile than rice paper. They're ripped by a single photograph dropped across our television screen: the bent arm of a Somali boy, every bone visible through withered flesh, each joint a knot. Follow the line of his shoulder, his neck, to his eye, and all apologies disintegrate, though there's no rage or reproach in his fixed stare. He can't see us, this faraway child. He can't imagine the food stuffed into our refrigerators. Our observation of him is a one-way conversation, the duration controlled by our thumb on a remote control button, and we desperately *want* it to be a story, a cautionary tale. Not real. Not contemporary. Not a mirror of our family's past or of its future.

It does no good to that boy on the flickering screen if we wait until he is dead, wait until all the children are gone and the adult populace is too defeated even to step aside for our news cameras and camouflage-dressed troops, before we commit to action.

❖

Food is very much on the mind of the village secretary in charge of equitably distributing food to Disaster and other children. She's a woman with strong arms and her own sleeping toddler secured on her back with a twisted shawl, a woman so driven by the heavy responsibility of her mission that she seems more vital than the rest of us, her skin more richly dark, her teeth whiter, her eyes less likely to miss something important. She speaks Tonga in low bursts, justifiably confident that anyone in the vicinity will strain to hear her words, and is all business in her negotiations with Ruben McKenzie, the local Save the Children administrator, who translates for my benefit.

She proposes that a number of village women participate in this program on a rotating basis, measuring out grain or weighing children for government records; they, too, should be afforded the luxury of an occasional meal, since lately some of them have passed out from hunger. Ruben should be clear, she adds, that this provision will not extend to her or to members of her governing committee, who, to avoid any suspicion of profiteering, have made themselves permanently ineligible for a ration.

Ruben, a handsome young man born and raised nearby, patiently explains that there's only a certain amount of food available; if more people partake, the portions will necessarily be smaller. The decision, however, is up to the woman and her colleagues.

She nods, one item on her agenda ticked off, and moves on. What about the Agency's pull-cart, she wants to know. When it isn't in use for this program, might she have permission to designate it for other purposes, such as transporting the sick to the airstrip? Otherwise, it will simply sit idle.

Once again Ruben confirms her authority, and once again the woman and the audience of recipients who watch this drama for entertainment are satisfied. There remains one final issue to be settled: will Ruben please find out and report on his next visit what will happen to the fifty-gallon tin drum, now on loan to store water, when the rains come back? The request is made casually, offhand, but no one present believes for an instant that there isn't already a specific task envisioned for this rusty object of foreign manufacture, a task that will, if humanly possible, be accomplished.

"Where does your water come from now?" I ask the woman, and am led nearly a mile down a path to the chalky expanse of what normally would be a river bottom. Into a small hole, a scrape in the dirt, there seeps a puddle of brown water. We stand around the perimeter in silence, for the shallowness, the precariousness, is self-evident, and eventually I look up at the secretary's face. She's frowning, thinking hard, absolutely determined to figure something out.

✣

The flight back to the capital is made without conversation. Even the bush pilot, a loquacious and good-natured American from Oregon, has been sobered into contemplation. The land beneath us is unworldly, pockmarked at regular intervals by what looks from the air like rivets protruding from the flat brown plain but are in fact termite mounds, each an identical masterpiece of conical engineering, the center of a fiercely demarcated territory. These are habitations impervious to drought, ideally suited to survive, even thrive, in Africa, and are the model for Zimbabwe's most famous modern invention: the VIP latrine, an odorless, low-maintenance device constructed throughout the country.

There's an unmistakable consonance of indigenous imagery and color, best perceived from a high vantage, an environmental harmony that's the product of thousands of years of natural adaptation, of trial and error, of successful evolutionary experiment. When it's interrupted, as in generations past, with the importation of non-native foodstuffs like maize—now considered by most Zimbabweans to be "traditional"—the results can be unpredictable. Millet and sorghum, the dietary staples of the region's ancient inhabitants, need less water to grow, but a learned preference for more recent tastes resists logic, and established patterns of consumption are slow to change. Some speculate that now that the hunger has become so great and people have been forced to eat the seeds they would otherwise save to plant, the choice of crops will begin to shift.

✤

Water is the chief concern, several hundred miles to the south in Mutema. I'm in a car with Gerry Salole, the Ethiopian-born Save the Children Regional Director, and we stop to ask directions of Jonathan Bhizeki, the elected local Pump Minder, through a rolled-down window. Only five of the thirty-five deep wells and one of the fourteen bore holes for which he bears responsibility have water, he tells us, and even they are rapidly becoming exhausted. For the twelve thousand people in and around this area of southeastern Zimbabwe, it's been a brutal, calamitous year. Not a single crop could be harvested, there is no food to buy in the shops, and no rain is expected until November. Handsome and distracted, Jonathan Bhizeki looks almost embarrassed, as if the sky's failure were his own.

Further up the road we visit the Chikwakwa Elementary School and talk with the principal. Dressed formally, as befits his position, in a tan tie beneath a maroon and white Argyle sweater, Clever Gwenzi is not hopeful. His father, born less than twenty kilometers away, has never in his lifetime seen such a drought. Economics eliminated the grade school children's lunch program, and as a result there are daily faintings and steep declines in attendance. It would cost an impossible 700 Zimbabwe dollars (about $140 U.S.) each week to reinstitute a daily meal for all 423 students. Money is especially tight. The World Bank, anxious that the last vestiges of Zimbabwe's former inclination toward socialism be abandoned, successfully urged the imposition of a token tuition charge for all grade levels. Equivalent to one U.S. dollar per year per child, this fee constitutes a burden to the poorest families, who have responded by sending only boys to classes. Too many of the girls, Clever Gwenzi regrets to say, have resorted to prostitution in order to eat.

As we drive up the hill away from Chikwakwa, we experience a small miracle: a two-minute rain shower. It's so surprising that Gerry stops the car and turns on the windshield wipers. Nothing happens. Though the odometer shows in excess of sixty thousand miles driven, no previous driver has had occasion to realize that the wipers don't work.

The rain stops as quickly as it began, and a moment later there's no evidence it ever happened—no puddles, no glistening surfaces. The land is so dry it has instantly inhaled every drop of moisture.

Our last stop is the community clinic, a rectangular cinder-block structure with a commanding view of the valley below and home to a resident physician and three nurses. The building shares a single well with the educational compound—and now with much of the general population. If that source of water fails, the doctor tells us, everything will close down within a day's time.

"How is the general health of the area?" Gerry inquires. Save the Children has operated here in the Middle Sabe region for years and has in fact contributed heavily to the construction of many of the newer buildings, creating a

[23]

particular responsibility, a special relationship. I've heard from several people an unsubstantiated but logical rumor that villages with an established bond to an international charity are at a greater than usual risk during hard times because the government, fully expecting that such communities will be assisted by enhanced donations from abroad, moves them down on the priority list of needy domestic cases. Unfortunately, Western philanthropic donations have dropped rather than increased in recent years—a phenomenon professional fund-raisers term "famine fatigue"—and the expectations are impossible to meet.

The health-care workers seem exhausted, defensive. They describe protein deficiency, pellagra, but vehemently deny having seen any cases of AIDS. Just send the medicine we require, they tell us. We'll take care of things from there.

In the dazzling African sunset, the stark white buildings stand in relief against a red-orange, cloudless sky, and not even the sound of birds intrudes upon the silence. There's a dying tree in the center of a circle of stones, a gesture toward landscaping. To change the subject, I ask the species, but no one knows. It's not indigenous.

"I had a farm in Africa," Gerry Salole quotes Isak Dinesen, and I quite understand the literary allusion. The romantic, European-viewed Africa of stampeding herds of wildebeest, endless frontier and solitude is seductive, much gentler than the parched bed of the Sabe River, studded with the decaying carcasses of animals who came to drink and found no moisture.

There are dozens of good reasons for us not to donate these days. "The economy," we complain, without being very specific. "And besides, I gave last year to fill-in-the-blank and look, nothing has changed." We exonerate ourselves with predictable scandals: the inflated salaries drawn by certain CEOs of philanthropic organizations, the percentage of every dollar that goes for vague "overhead," the imminence of closer urgencies where our gift might have a more direct and monitorable impact. And then, of course, there's the suspicion that conditions are exaggerated by those who seek to tap our sympathy. We wait, as Peter Applebome writes in the *New York Times* (December 13, 1992), for television to make "the world's suffering as inescapable as a four-alarm fire next door."

"You see those starving kids on TV," he quotes Lee Hoskins, a 59-year-old route salesman for a dairy company who lives in Villa Hills, Kentucky. "And you think, 'How could we not do this?'"

Indeed, media coverage is the key to a national sympathy agenda. Simultaneously proud of our softheartedness and of our skepticism, we want proof—death counts, weight-loss graphs, raw film footage—before we react. If we give at all, it must be to the best place, the neediest victim, the furthest gone. A Somalia becomes deserving of our benevolent invasion only after it's certifiably wrecked.

❖

During one of the famines that raked the Horn of Africa in the past ten years, there was a community in which starving human beings and starving baboons were reduced to competing directly against each other for food. Baboons are wily, agile and hard to discourage, but desperate, the people devised a plan. A lone female baboon was ambushed, brought back to the village, and skinned alive. Her screams echoed into the hills, and soon a ring of alarmed baboons approached the periphery of the invisible line that traditionally divided the territory of men and women from that of animals. The tortured baboon was untied, and, blind with pain, she ran frantically in the direction of her home.

The sight, they say, was terrible for a person to see, even worse for another baboon. Unrecognizable, the victim was the embodiment of horror: the familiar inverted to nightmare. Some baboons fled, others attacked with teeth and claws until, finally, the thing was still. But from that day forward, villagers had no rivals in their quest for the few remaining fruits and roots and grains that survived in the region. All the baboons had gone away.

❖

The average Zimbabwean citizen is not psychologically prepared for calamity on the scale forecast. This country, formerly the British colony of Southern Rhodesia, is traditionally a major player in "the bread basket of Africa." It normally has a healthy, varied economy, a sufficiency of what's necessary, and so the population is schooled in optimism. "Rain will no doubt come," I was told again and again by both urban and rural people. "It always has. It must."

But, according to meteorologists, it won't, without a miracle. And even with ideal weather, no crops will be ready for harvest before late May. In the interim there are several crucial needs, none of them impossible to meet. Existing wells must be deepened, at an average total cost of $600 U.S. each, or new ones dug, for $3000. Trucks must be either leased or bought to transport emergency food supplies. Supplementary feeding programs must be minimally sustained at current levels, and some goats and cattle must be kept alive through the dry summer and fall in order to form the core of commercial livestock herds in the future.

These things are matters of life and death, and take priority over other pressing social issues—and there are many. The minimum weekly wage in Zimbabwe is roughly equivalent to the price of nine Wimpie double cheeseburgers in Masvingo, the fourth largest city, where government lower-income housing costs on the average $100 a month. Bus transportation to and from work, so slow and intermittent that almost everyone attempts to hitch rides with passing motorists, runs at about a dollar a day. There's an unspoken, mostly unacknowledged, antagonism between the haves and the have-nots, evidenced by the fact that most wealthy homeowners hire poor men to stand guard at the entrance to their property all night, every night.

And yet Zimbabwe, even with roughly half of its total population officially in need of food assistance, is the success story of a region that includes Mozambique, Angola, Malawi and Zambia—all far worse off in one way or another. Zimbabwe has the political infrastructure, the network of good roads, the system of dependable communications to be stable, but not if it must impoverish itself in order merely to survive, not if it must buy food with money earmarked for crucial economic development.

Harare has become home to a whole community of professional relief workers, veterans of emergency campaigns in Sudan, Mali, Ethiopia and the Western Sahara. They know each other's agendas, socialize in the same circles, speak a similar idiom of grant proposals and dramatic cost analyses. A public information officer from Uruguay stopped me in the hall of the U.N. mission. "You look familiar," she said pleasantly. "What other crises have you covered lately?"

There are currently 641 foreign nongovernmental organizations (NGOs) registered in Zimbabwe, each with its own national specialty—the British and Scandinavians concentrate on water, Americans on food. Some, like CARE,

Save the Children, the Red Cross and Africair, are working directly and practically to mitigate the current emergency, but their ability to disperse funds depends upon consistent patterns of giving, maintained with the repetition of demand. Certain countries have stellar records of assistance: Norway, with a population of four million people, last year came up with $20 million in aid. However, if the font of generosity dries up along with the water, if habitually forthcoming donors get discouraged or redirect their resources to a Bosnia or Afghanistan or Bangladesh, southern Africa will face alone and with almost no self-generated capital a food and water blight of proportions unprecedented in this century.

❖

Americans like me are always "discovering" grand-scale poverty and being famously shocked by the magnitude of it. Most of the time, we flirt with awareness, gulp it in sound bites from the network anchors or register it from newspaper photographs staged to produce the maximum horror. We shudder, we recoil, we even write off the occasional check or buy an overpriced ticket to a benefit, thus entertaining ourselves and doing good simultaneously. But in general, distant disasters are treated like rumors, lacking the immediacy of fear, the focus of personal danger or entanglement. They're our problem only when we allow them time to capture our attention, and then, with the ardor of converts who've just received revelation, we often become righteous and zealous. We accost our friends with dire statistics, censure their ignorance, insist upon their full-blown involvement. We love to manipulate simplistic financial analogies: "$25 billion—roughly equal to the amount Americans spend on beer or the amount spent on the world's militaries every 13 days—would provide adequate nutrition, clean water, basic health care and primary education for all the world's children," proclaims a 1992 UNICEF report, as if in response readers will instantly be transformed into teetotalers.

True, a few persist to batter at the wall of tragedy, repeatedly crashing against it, but for the rest of us, burnout, disappointment and frustration are merely a matter of when.

We expect results, a bang for our bucks, a return on our emotional and financial investment. If we have the option of looking the other way, usually, eventually, we exercise it.

❖

The road that led me to Zimbabwe was circuitous, without plan or ambition. It unfolded, as with most events in my life, as a series of virtual free associations, the sequence obvious only in retrospect. In 1971 I adopted a child who turned out to have been prenatally damaged by fetal alcohol syndrome. After a decade of denying his problem, I discovered its medical designation at about the same time that my wife, Louise Erdrich, began to encourage me to write. For lack of any other viable response, I authored an account of our son's life, and as a result of confessing my utter failure to improve Abel's impairments, I perversely became publicly associated with child welfare. That misplaced notoriety led to my joining the governing board of Save the Children, and at the conclusion of the second meeting I attended in Westport, Connecticut, a program officer back from the field made a presentation about the long and underreported drought in Southern Africa. "If only," he concluded his remarks, "we could get wider press coverage and awareness, we might be able to better prepare these national economies and avoid some of the misery that's happened elsewhere under similar conditions."

Until that moment I had found it hard to justify my participation in Save the Children. I lacked a background either in development or in philanthropy, and other than having years before been a $12-a-month sponsor of one of the

Foundation's clients, I seemed to have little to offer by way of contribution. But I did have training in anthropology, and I had written columns for the op-ed pages of several big city newspapers, so I volunteered to spend part of July in Zimbabwe and then try to publish my observations.

I got the prescribed inoculations, cleared my schedule and called my press contacts to describe my plan. The first question I was asked turned out to be telling: "Is it a sexy drought?" one senior editor wanted to know.

"Sexy?"

"Sell it to me," he said. "Why is this one different? What don't I know about it? We've done the sympathy bit, and readers' eyes glaze over. Jazz it up, and we'll give you the ink."

❖

Weeks later I try to explain this attitude—and the related big business of charity appeals—to Mark Nyahada, a local Save the Children deputy administrator. We sit with a small, tired group at the table of a guest house located deep within a government-run oasis—an agricultural station with working wells and sprinklers, a dot of verdant green upon the red and tan lower veldt near the Mozambican border. A few miles to the north on a barren plateau, the community of Muusha is slowly starving, and a few miles to the southwest sprawls the refugee camp of Tongogara.

"I don't understand it," Mark says, frowning. He's a muscular, energetic, solution-oriented person, someone with no tolerance for foolishness. "We don't need so much, but what we need, we need. Where is the help?"

I reach for the ubiquitous jar of coffee "substitute," sucrose and artificial creamer already mixed in, that, together with Coca-Cola and orange squash, seems to be the beverage of choice in rural Zimbabwe.

"Imagine receiving your mail in the morning," I suggest. "One or two personal letters, a few bills, and then a bunch of envelopes with return addresses of famous people—movie stars, ex-presidents. Inside each one is a professionally produced solicitation that strives to interest you in a particular agenda: right to life, freedom of choice, American Indians, the election of a candidate who promises to make the country better, cancer research, kidney replacement, the protection of the environment. The texts are engineered by marketing experts—advertising executives with degrees in psychology— trained to grab the reader with an opening sentence and wring a few dollars from a vulnerable conscience. Half the time you don't even open up these letters, just toss them in the trash so you don't have to think about everything you can't change."

"How do such people know your address?"

"Maybe a year ago you read an article about . . . AIDS," I answer. "Or you knew someone who was sick and you looked for a way to show your sympathy, so you sent a contribution to support a hospice. The hospice needed money, so it sold its mailing list of donors to another charity, and they did the same thing. Soon you're on everybody's computer as being good for $50 or $100, and the machines take over. There's only one of you and a thousand deserving causes. You can drown in them. They become a blur, all wanting your attention and your spare change, like a street lined with beggars. Most people shut their eyes, close their ears, speed up, run."

❖

To a new arrival, "camp" must seem a bizarre designation for Tongogara, a colonial plantation turned refugee center near the eastern Zimbabwe border where forty-two thousand displaced Mozambicans wait behind a steel fence—some since the mid-1980s—for their country's particularly vicious civil war to wind down. Each moving vehicle, each running child, is announced by a trail of the fine bronze dust that eventually coats everyone and everything with the same earthy skin.

This place, described to me as "the Hilton hotel of refugee camps," is a grid of red-orange mud-and-thatch huts, schools and bureaucracy. It's efficiently, if somewhat dictatorially, run by David Malambo, a corpulent administrator who wears three college rings, a chronometer watch, a cowboy shirt with snaps instead of buttons and an ornate Texas belt buckle. He presides from an office decorated with thirty-three hand-printed aphorisms, inspirational sayings such as, "I am blessed and I confer blessings on others." I sit before his huge desk, blasted by his wide, constant smile and booming laugh, while his shrewd, intelligent eyes, belying the more outrageous aspects of his public persona, fix me to my chair.

I listen, spellbound, as Malambo unfolds one enormous hand and counts off his NGO wish list, finger by finger. His top priority, along with the drilling of additional wells, is the installation of a camp-wide loudspeaker system so that his frequent announcements will be instantly accessible to all residents, direct and without the confusion of reinterpretation. The donations he seeks from Western donors range from vials of sulfa drugs to a basketball ("for the 22,000 children") to a renewal of his personal subscription to *National Geographic*.

Recently the camp almost had its first full-time doctor: a Hindu from India, trained in Great Britain, was willing to come, but the appointment fell through. It does boast a brand-new Dewey-decimal-driven library, built with Italian lira, that houses, between the "Silence" signs, books like *The Economic History of Canada* and seventeen copies of an introductory calculus paperback published in 1978. The collection, in general, easily replicates the back-room bookshelves of half the people I know: once-used college textbooks, old issues of *Time* magazine, Sharper Image catalogues whose high-tech gadgetry in this desperate African context must seem the farfetched stuff of science fiction.

For years now, the stream of refugees has continued to flow through the gates: hungry, worn-out, disheartened people, struggling across the parched landscape of a *Road Warrior* film. Each person has a story, as tragic and archetypal at its heart as an epic novel: the search for a lost son or daughter; widows; unaccompanied orphans, some too young to relate any information about themselves beyond a nickname. When there's enough film, their mug-shot photographs are distributed throughout the camp in hopes that someone, somewhere, will recognize a face.

Within sight of the former plantation owner's swimming pool, now padlocked and dry, today's cluster of displaced persons sit dazed on packed dirt, "guarded" by a contingent of bored soldiers. Most speak a dialect related to Shona, the predominant tribal language of Zimbabwe, and so I'm able to communicate through Mark Nyahada. He's come to Tongogara today to supervise a newly inaugurated program, run cooperatively by Save the Children, the Zimbabwe government and a U.S. team of psychologists and social workers from Duke University, aimed both at reuniting separated family members and caring for the youngest witnesses to unspeakable violence.

"Some of these children," Mark tells me in his very British accent, "have seen terrible things. They've been forced to kill their parents. Made to carry ammunition across enemy lines. Seen people locked inside houses that were then set on fire."

In the late morning torpor of the reception area, where the only sounds are the buzz of flies and the low conversation of soldiers, it's hard to imagine such atrocities—until I see the eyes of one little boy about ten years old. His expression is exhausted, devoid of curiosity, matching the listlessness of the elderly woman beside him.

Mark notices the direction of my gaze. "That's his grandmother," he tells me. "His mother is still somewhere in Mozambique. They hoped the father would be here, but so far we haven't been able to locate him."

Mark beckons, the boy comes over, and in the custom of

men conversing, we squat face to face. Unmoving, the grandmother stares through us as if watching another place and time. There are stretched holes in the lobes of her ears where jewelry once dangled. Mark estimates that she's no more than fifty, yet she appears to me much older.

There's nothing childlike about this boy, nothing playful or energetic. Like so many people I meet in these camps, he has about him an air of distilled dignity, as if, denied every other possession, he has quietly retained possession of himself.

Mark translates the story the boy elects to tell us, and it is, within this inhumane context, undramatic, even typical. Yes, he's gone days without eating. Yes, he and his grandmother have walked shoeless from a long distance. Yes, he's hoping to find his father, who ran away from their village some time ago to avoid execution for the crime of being brother-in-law to the wrong person. The boy is neither rushed nor especially sorry for himself, just tired. He's never been to school but clearly he's intelligent, a survivor. If it weren't for his size, for the absence of lines on his face, I'd think I was in the presence of a resigned, mature man.

Mark promises that he'll circulate the boy's photograph throughout the several refugee centers scattered along the frontier; he'll even send it along to his counterpart in Malawi, where more than one million Mozambicans have fled. Perhaps a relative will see it and contact the authorities. Perhaps the story will have a benign resolution.

The boy nods, then rejoins his grandmother. Mark and I

stand, brush off our knees and walk towards our Toyota. We're running behind schedule, late for a meeting. Before I get into the car, however, I turn back for one last look. The boy is cradled in his grandmother's thin arms. His mouth is at her empty breast.

❖

Bad luck has created this predicament, bad luck and the incessant meddling of foreign governments—who've lost interest in southern Africa now that the cold war is history. At one end of the looping line of connection is constant pain, and at the other is the possibility of carefree joy. At the far extreme stands that prematurely old little boy of Tongogara. A million options away are we, am I. Thrown together by chance—at an arbitrary moment in time, we found ourselves occupying the same place—we beheld each other, registered our similarities. For every child like him, there are 100,000 more I don't happen to encounter, and for every man like me, there are millions he can't imagine, yet we stare across the chasm, each trying briefly to fathom the other's life.

No greater distance separates us than this: he stays, I leave. But not entirely alone. I have a daughter about his age, a shining girl whose last act before my trip was to empty her bulldog bank and send her birthday money along for me to give away. To her, on some unspoiled level, she and the boy I've just met have the obvious potential of contemporaries, of playmates. She has not yet learned to tolerate injustice as inevitable, to become defeated in advance by the enormous odds against making a difference through reaching out. For her, what's directly before her eyes is still visible, and the syllogism is quite simple. They need. I have. Therefore, I give, in order to reestablish a fair balance.

As Mark and I drive north on a two-lane road, past grass-roofed villages and straggling goats that seem more bone than flesh, the faces of two children—who will never meet—superimpose and fix permanently in my imagination.

❖

The United States is about to spend a million Zimbabwe dollars to implement an elephant preservation program in Gonarezhou National Park, far to the south in the most parched area of the country—a scheme that involves the digging of bore hole wells exclusively for the watering of animals.

Gibson Lampha, the U.S. ambassador, explains the mechanics to me. An affable, tanned career diplomat, he's lined the walls of his Harare office with watercolors of trout flies and many photographs of his family posed amid the rushing streams and green mountains of Mono County, California.

"Sometimes I think I'm fighting two governments, this one and my own," he confides. "You take advantage of what's available—like the African Elephant Preservation Act. It passed Congress in 1989 and is administered by the Department of Fish and Wildlife. There's $200,000 left in the kitty—that's the million Zimb dollars. Unfortunately it can't be used for human beings, except peripherally."

My face must have registered indignation.

"Hold on," he says. "It's not an either/or. The U.S. has donated $120 million for food in Zimbabwe alone," Lampha tells me. "We've just upped the imports of wheat, maize, sugar and soybeans to fifteen million tons via South African and Mozambican ports."

"Will thirsty people who are prohibited from using the elephants' wells realize that?" I wonder aloud, recalling a story I've twice heard related with great sarcasm. Supposedly Coca-Cola presented two grants in the same public ceremony: $5 million for wildlife, and $1 million for human beings. The priority did not go unnoticed.

Lampha shakes his head to indicate I'm allowing myself to be sidetracked. "Bankers here are looking at a growth rate of -8 percent. George Bush is in trouble back home with a +2 to 3 percent, so imagine the impact on the Zimbabwe economy. Local manufacturers get 60 percent of their business input from agriculture, especially cotton. They export to the Gap and Banana Republic. Each textile worker typically supports six to eight people, but without foreign currency . . ."

Lampha removes his silver-framed glasses and rubs his eyes. I'm impressed with his candor, his command of statistics. He's just the kind of capable, compassionate representative I hadn't expected to find appointed in the legacy of the Reagan and Bush administrations.

"Zimbabwe has a 40 percent inflation rate due to the Structural Adjustment Program," he continues. "It's the size of Montana with not a single large natural body of water. The big lakes are man-made, and the water table is dropping. I've used all my discretionary funds for water programs—$240,000 out of a total of $250,000. And the rains are no help. Lots fell in the game park in the far west and a sufficient amount around Harare itself, but little where the farmers need it."

"So what's the answer?"

"Look," Lampha says. "This is a nation that's played the game right, by our own and the world's rules. It has the setup for a true modern economy. President Mugabe has worked hard for peace in Mozambique because he needs stable ports and because he want the refugees to have a place to go home to. The education and medical care programs are well managed, a model of family planning—the average number of children per family has declined from 3.6 to 2.9, all with government support. And now the country's screwed because of drought and refugees. Plus AIDS, of course. A doctor I talked to in Zaka yesterday informs me that it's become the number one cause of death in certain age categories."

❖

Overflow refugees at Tongogara this season have been rerouted to Chambuta, a new camp Mark and I visit along the bed of what, in a normal year, is the wide Runde River, just across from Gonarezhou. Now full beyond capacity at 20,000 people—up from 6,000 in January—Chambuta is divided into thirteen "villages," though two of them so far lack the most rudimentary shelter. The Zimbabwean government, reeling under its own deprivations, has provided sufficient water and food rations, but there is no disguising the utter bleakness of the place, the stark, wintry desert, the barrenness. It is, quite literally, the end of the road.

Most of the 700 people who arrive daily, the natty young director, Israel Chokowenga, reports, are without clothing, confused, disoriented, sick and always thirsty. Drought, not war, is their "presenting problem," and everywhere there's manifest evidence of misery. My eyes stray to the operational flow chart on the wall behind his desk, and I marvel at the attention paid to specifying bureaucracy.

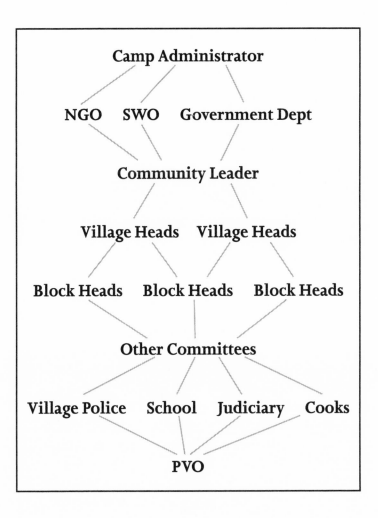

"What would help?" I ask Chokowenga, and he replies without hesitation.

"It takes people three to seven days to walk to the border," he says. "They're weak, disheartened, but still another week elapses before they're eligible to register for the supplementary food program. It's awful for everyone, but especially for the children. If only . . ." He bridges his fingers, sighs at the impossibility of what he is about to say. "If only each child could have a glass of milk each day they remain at the border. Even the adults, too, to tide them over."

To kill time, I walk out the door of the reception center. Passing before my line of sight, a girl, one leg stiff and too short, lugs a can for water toward an open spigot. As she hobbles, she leaves odd footprints: the left is as it should be, the right is only flexed toes. There are flies and more flies, ever seeking the moisture that resides at the corners of a person's eyes or mouth. Many at Chambuta seem to lack the energy or the will to blink. No one even begs.

I cross a dirt path and immediately come upon an undersized boy, hot with fever. He lies unattended on the ground, his head propped against a canvas pack, bisected with the stripe of shade cast by a thorn tree whose branches have been stripped for firewood. Here at last is the immediate context I've previously managed to avoid: the boy from television and me, alone together, one-on-one. If he is to receive help at this moment, it's up to me to provide or summon it, to broadcast his distress, to identify and activate the person in charge.

Because I'm a visitor, instantly identifiable by my paler skin and expensive clothing, my pause draws attention. Israel Chokowenga sees me from his window and quickly joins me at the boy's side. He sends for a health aide, and while we wait I pick up a pamphlet that's blowing along the ground. On its cover is an illustration of a highly stylized Satan—horns, goatee and pitchfork, the works.

"A Christian group left those here," Chokowenga offers by way of embarrassed explanation.

I glance at the text, which, in English, exhorts the reader to avoid such temptations as dancing, drinking and heavy petting in preparation for an hospitable reception into paradise. Those who published the leaflet presumably intended that the devil appear wicked and menacing, but my guess is that to these Shona-speaking Mozambicans, he simply looks like a European.

"Measles," the health-care worker pronounces when she arrives. "Or malnutrition. His family was here before, so they must be close by—probably getting the day's ration." She produces a yellow identification card for the boy and points to a check mark to show that he has received an injection of penicillin, but my glance strays to the spot where his date of birth is recorded.

"This can't be right," I object. "It would make him eleven years old, and he's not more than three."

The aid worker and Chokowenga look dubious. Starving children often appear younger than their years.

"I have a three-year-old," I insist. "I know."

In fact, the card refers to an older brother, located with his father near the pump. There's a flurry of activity, and the correct data is produced. The little boy was born on Valentine's Day 1989, ten days before my daughter. His name is Anthony. His ailment is "Unknown."

Roused by the presence of a crowd, by the buzz of conversation, Anthony has opened his eyes, found his father and closed them again. He's unaware that he's become something of a celebrity, found by a chance spotlight that may or may not improve his odds for survival. I look at the shallow rise and fall of his chest and think of all besides medicine to which he should be entitled: plumped pillows and ginger ale and chicken soup, fairy tales told in a soothing voice, tiptoed checks at midnight, cool hands against his brow, the promise that health will return, that a full life lies ahead.

Another boy, tiny, frowning, squats beside the administration building. He seems deep in thought, protected by a concentration I've never seen in one so young. Again we seem caught together within a frozen frame. In my backpack I have a paper bag filled with inexpensive American Indian beadwork jewelry—medallions and earrings—I've brought from Montana to give as presents, but somehow, so far, I've never found the appropriate occasion. In the places I've visited, the objects seemed too gay, too frivolous, but now instinctively I set the whole sack in the dirt at the boy's feet. Maybe the contents will make him smile.

His startle reflex causes me to draw back. Without altering his posture, he manages to hunker down even tighter than before, clasping his arms more closely about his knees, ducking his head deeper into his chest, a block of stone, a house with one room and room for only one. I'm reminded of tales of refugees who run for cover when their pictures are taken because the flash of light is too reminiscent of times when they were under artillery fire. The paper bag remains where I put it, unasked for, unopened.

On the other side of the administration building, next to parking spaces demarcated by carefully aligned rocks, is Chambuta's unofficial greeter. He's dressed in a knitted beige ski cap, a tattered Hard Rock Café T-shirt and khaki pants, has advanced glaucoma in both cloudy eyes and bears the unreadable expression of a man in the midst of a long interior monologue. Yet, equipped with a branch bowed by a piece of wire, a hollow gourd for resonance and a twig as a dancing hammer, he's making music.

I tap him on the shoulder, point to my cassette player and gesture a question: may I record? He smiles, nods and begins his song anew. People see me holding up my little black machine and wander over to watch. His melodic voice is pitched high, the callused fingers of one hand slide deftly along the wire, varying chords. Verse follows verse, and when he's done I rewind, press play. The man, who has stood perfectly still while singing, now does a shuffling, barefoot dance to his own tune, and the audience approves, clapping in time. On tape the music is somehow more worthy of listening, compelling as a radio, the stuff of capital cities and official government networks. As Mark and I get back into our car and drive out the gate, the singer remains surrounded by teenagers, who pay close attention as he demonstrates his art. I turn to wave, and the last thing I see is him handing over his instrument, placing the hands of an eager boy in the right positions on the improvised string.

We head north, looking for a shortcut to the main highway, and I harbor no illusions about the import of my visit to these camps. At best I was an agent of coincidence, a random microphone that temporarily raised the volume of several voices, a weather front passing high above that dropped a hint of rain here and there, and then blew away.

✤

Of the recent atrocities reported from the Mozambican front, one story stands out: a group of boys armed with automatic weapons appeared in a neighboring community. Swiftly they surrounded a group of local children no older than themselves and shot them. When asked why, one fourteen-year-old explained that the children of that village had been kindly treated by adults, rarely beaten and fed daily. The attacking boys were indignant, jealous, so they evened the score. In their experience of the world, a lack of suffering was a sufficient reason to die.

With such events fresh in their ears and eyes, it's little wonder that nearly 3.5 million mostly rural Mozambicans have walked away from their homes and livelihoods; 1.5 million of them have deserted their country and, somehow finding the physical stamina to endure the trek, have wound up at refugee camps in surrounding Malawi, Zambia or Zimbabwe. In Malawi they now number the equivalent of ten percent of the total national population. Officially they have no money, no opportunity to petition for immigrant status, so they suffer the occasional vocational training program, collect firewood from the stub of every tree left in the wide radius of a day's walk, and sleep. Among them now are children just reaching adolescence who've never known a previous life.

Every day I spend in southeastern Zimbabwe pushes back the boundary of deprivation I believed human beings could endure. In the camps there is an unrelieved sense of waiting, but it's a waiting bereft of expectation, a queue so stalled that no one remembers what was supposed to be at the end. It's a waiting for the fickleness of climate, the eventuality of death, the unlikely news of civil peace, the abrupt interruption of food or drink. It hums with a passive inertia, a kind of dull concession that no individual act or thought can effect the outcome.

❖

There's a huge bathtub in my room at the Flamboyant Hotel in Masvingo. Like the "Right of Admission Reserved" sign above the establishment's grand entrance—in the thirteen years since Rhodesia became Zimbabwe, no one has gotten around to removing the two screws that hold the old banner of segregation in place—it seems an anomalous relic in a city about to run out of water. Dirty and fatigued, I yearn for a bath and automatically dump the contents of my pockets on a bureau as I prepare to disrobe. Four quarters. A year's tuition at the Chikwakwa School. I can't bring myself to turn the taps. Earlier in the day, I've sworn to myself never to complain about anything ordinary again. Mere discomfort and inconvenience are signs of bounty, for to be aware of them suggests a familiarity with their opposites. No one would begrudge me a bath, and I feel no pride or righteousness in foregoing it for one night, but private abundance, the beckon of warm immersion, is simply out of the question. I need greater distance, a dulling of short-term memory. And I know that will come.

The next morning Gerry Salole must attend a meeting, and I find myself, for the first time on this trip, with nothing scheduled. Sipho Ndovlu, a deputy director of Save the Children's operation, suggests that we visit the country's major tourist attraction, only about twenty miles away. Great Zimbabwe, the House of Stone, is an enigmatic, fortresslike edifice perched on high rocks—a citadel or a religious shrine, no one seems quite sure, laboriously constructed out of boulders long before the arrival of any European. It's likely that the Shona used it as a refuge against the invasion from the south of the Ndebele Tribe—Sipho's people—centuries past.

Sipho has never before climbed to the top, and as we ascend we make much of his latter-day scaling of the ramparts although, possessed of a sweet and beatific smile, he seems the most unlikely of warriors. Together we wander the site, pass from roofless room to room, clamoring over displaced rocks and doing our best to avoid the concession stands and cultural shows—tribal dancing, fortune telling, singing—geared for the busloads of South African tourists. Despite its commercialization, Great Zimbabwe remains a place of dignity, of antiquity. Everywhere we go there arches above us the pale blue African sky, opening and opening and opening into endless space.

❖

Groundwater is counted as private property in Zimbabwe, and so those with means and luck need not experience the drought directly, though the nearby reservoir of Lake Kyle is widely reputed to be at .3 percent of capacity, and local "dry farms" (that is, farms that depend on rain rather than tapping the depleting aquifer with sprinklers) have produced no crops at all for two growing seasons. Still, some Zimbabweans continue to behave as though this were a normal year. There are more than a dozen private golf courses still kept green in Harare, only three hours to the north, and behind their iron gates, the gardens of suburban houses bloom with manicured avocado trees and bougainvillea. Here and there in the countryside, perfume rises from orange groves irrigated by the deepest bore holes, and the capital's Holiday Inn has posted no water conservation signs. It is as though, as Gerry Salole has ironically commented, someone had invented a machine to draw the oxygen out of the air and sell it to the rich, as though the reality of the current national disaster must strike each citizen individually.

Last to feel the effects may well be the residents of Avondale, a suburb of gracious homes and well-stocked shopping centers. In late afternoon its shaded lanes are regularly bordered by lines of maids, gardeners, security guards and cooks, their features set into expressions of what I interpret as "pre-anger." They're waiting for the infrequent bus to bring them far south to the crowded "high-density" townships where flood lamps installed atop high steel poles are kept illuminated throughout night, their glare obscuring the view of even a full African moon. As my hosts cart me around town, I feel a keen accusation in those looks. In all the time I've been in Zimbabwe, in urban or in rural areas, I've seen just one person of European origin in such a crowd, but no one else seems to find this remarkable. I can only conclude that the practice of inequity is so common, its resentment so constant and ordinary a drone, that it blankets individual perception.

I'm offered an undiluted perspective on this stratified society by a blue-suited business executive whose ancestors migrated from England generations ago and who professes to be completely "of Africa." We meet in her downtown Harare office, where I've arrived with a notebook but no writing implement.

"Take it with you and you're dead," she jokes, lending me her pen. "And I think we can spare the water for one cup of coffee."

We've agreed in advance that I will not mention her name or place of business, but otherwise "anything goes," so I begin with the question of rigid class structure. I'm the second foreigner this year to mention to her the ethnic makeup of the street-side queues.

"I thought the first man was talking out of the back of his neck," she says. "People of different cultures just don't mix."

But "racialism is alive and well," she goes on to explain,

though of a more benevolent nature than under the old apartheid system in South Africa. Even now, the only reason the wealthy here don't simply close up their homes and go to Europe for several months to wait out the drought is because their servants would be left "high and dry."

A self-described "flaming liberal," she blames government corruption and bad planning for much of the country's economic problems, noting that "we've gone from white fat cats to black fat cats, but before, at least, the system worked. There was integrity." Plus, the large commercial farms were more efficient. "Village people are not stupid, but they're ignorant," she observes. "They have no money, and their fields are too remote from the marketplace." This brings to mind a similar observation by Gibson Lampha. "It goes against liberal thinking," he told me, "but this country might work best with large commercial farms. The farmers, black or white, would take care of the needs of their laborers."

I return the woman's pen and thank her for her time. Her self-satisfaction has been oddly refreshing in its own way: finally I have an outlet for my anger. She has even said, unbidden, that some of her best friends are black, that sometimes, when visiting in African neighborhoods, she actually forgets she is white. Sure you do, I think to myself, and instantly recognize a parallel smugness of my own. Her attitudes, though less efficiently disguised, are similar to those of many Americans of her generation, and are probably even relatively enlightened by colonial standards. She is no more oblivious to the hardship in the surrounding countryside than, say, her counterpart in Kansas City is uninformed about poverty conditions on the Pine Ridge or Rosebud reservations. Her air of assumed superiority, of weary noblesse oblige, is certainly part of the heritage that resulted in the current African sociopolitical crisis, but her humiliation and deportation wouldn't solve much. It wouldn't bring rain. It wouldn't bring peace to Mozambique.

❖

It's hard to imagine a place more remote from the glass and steel high-rises of downtown Harare than the half-built and deserted public granary in Binga, a two-hour Cessna flight to the northwest where, in the company of the scholarly and thoughtful Chris Eldridge, Regional Director of Save the Children/U.K., I listen to the sorry report of an aptly named group: the Grinding Committee. Fuel has become so expensive that it's no longer profitable to operate the sleek new British-financed milling machine, and in any case there is no grain to grind.

The members of the Committee, all senior men, treat each other with great formality and respect. Their job seems to be to talk, to debate, to worry, to shake their heads. In the peculiar division of labor that I witnessed sporadically throughout the southern Africa bush, village males are sedentary observers and females toil, all leisure time illicitly stolen. It's the women of Binga who must walk five hours each way to collect water, the women who plant and sell the vegetables, who haul the wheat, the women who cut grass to pay for water and then accept whatever price for grain the Grinding Committee has set. There's nothing subtle about the patriarchy. A man signals, and immediately a woman rushes forward with the guest register for us to sign. She curtsies to each male present, averts her eyes and opens the book to a blank page.

The one nutritional hope, Chris Eldridge explains as our jeep bumps along a rough path hacked through dense forest, is the promise of free meat from a government-sponsored "cull" of elephants, antelope and crocodile by the Communal Area Management Program for Indigenous Resources (CAMPIR). This is expected to yield approximately six hundred tons of animals, which will translate into seventy tons of jerky (known here as biltong) and add much-needed protein to the local diet.

❖

On the flight back to the United States, my mind races, searching for some action, some call to arms, some original and efficacious idea in response to what I've seen. I tilt between the equally useless poles of helplessness and arrogance, of shrugging my shoulders and of changing my life. What is the appropriate path between wanting to help, on the one hand, and being defeated in the ambition by having no idea how, on the other?

The answer, I realize, begins with empathy based at the most individual level. It's too easy to forget the picture of a crowd, no matter how miserable. We don't think of our parents, of our children, as a group, but as specific people, each with his or her own personality, perspective and face. We must see through the burning, thirsty forest and find a tree to nurture, to water during the dry season so that it will provide shade in a later year. We must give as if to ourselves— automatically and practically, without the demand of gratitude or closure.

To be fortunate is, in a deep moral sense, to be obliged. Confusion is no excuse; doing something, even if mistakes are made, will help, especially in the early stages of trouble. And even from far away, our contributions can be specifically designated, if we make the effort to inform ourselves. In Zimbabwe, for instance, $1 will send a little girl to school for a year. $140 will buy a week's worth of lunches for four hundred students. $600 invested now will deepen an existing well, thus sustaining a whole community until the rains return, permitting people to stay independent rather than swelling the rolls of those forced to become internal refugees.

I close my eyes; twenty-two hours of flying to go, and yet the distance is not so easily re-achieved. Having seen Chambuta and Chunga, I will never be quite so far away as I used to be. Before leaving I've made the obvious, easy gesture: lightened my load by giving away for distribution most of the clothes I brought along, together with the Zimbabwe money I haven't spent. In the luxury of the British Air 747, I sit next to a Parisian computer engineer who visited the capital for a mere twelve hours. "*C'est un pays incroyable, non?*" he asks of me, and I know he's thinking of Harare's Fort Worth skyline, the clean broad avenues, the deferential politeness. On his lap the travel guide is open to Victoria Falls, the tourist attraction every European I've met in Zimbabwe has chastised me for missing.

"*C'est vrai, ça,*" I agree, but my thoughts are of Muusha, that hamlet on a plateau in southeastern Zimbabwe where I met the other side of fear.

She is short, wraps her head in a colorful torn scarf and is on her way to a funeral. Her laughter and her anger seem to alternate, to pulse against each other. She wears a ripped gray cardigan and flat blue plastic shoes, unlaced, and she's proud, straightforward, brave and crazed. Her companion, a man whose smile seems too broad, too unwavering to be normal, enthusiastically supports everything she says.

[64]

A businessman, she explains in emphatic English, the one who ran the shop that ran out of food a week ago, drank a cup of bad water the day before, too thirsty to boil it first. Naturally the diarrhea was awful—that was to be expected—but to die so quickly? This was not a good sign. It seemed almost too coincidental, too similar to what had happened to the two children last Thursday. She's worried, she admits it, and asks if we would like to observe a case of pellagra brought on by malnutrition. Foreigners are always impressed by such sights. The sick woman is in the house just down the lane. She won't mind our intrusion. Perhaps then we would talk to whoever it is that might be asked to send a little cornmeal.

In some respects Muusha is a model Shona community, the beneficiary of expatriate philanthropic attention and subsidy. There is the clinic, the woman explains, and there, those abandoned buildings? That had once been a large barn before the cattle starved. And look at the view. Foreign aid inspectors always remark about the way the land stretches west toward the mountains. Didn't I want to take a photograph so that I could show my family back home the beauty of this country?

I didn't bring a camera, but I did have a question. What will eventually happen, I ask the woman, who clearly has other things to do than talk to me. Will people leave, move to cities, join others in one of the five refugee camps Zimbabwe has established for Mozambicans who've fled across the border?

Leave? She's shocked, appalled at the idea. We would never leave our land.

But what if the last wells go dry and no more money is donated to dig them deeper? What if, as predicted, there will soon be no water?

Then we'll die, she says evenly, her eyes averted up the hill to the sad obligation for which we have already made her late. The man at her side—her brother? her husband? her son?—smiles agreement. Yes, he nods, indeed we'll die.

She turns back to me, too polite a hostess to terminate our conversation without some sign on my part of mutual conclusion.

"Thank you for your time," I say to release her.

Good. She takes her leave by the appropriate local custom, bowing slightly from the waist, wishing me health and gently clapping her hands together in the imitation of applause.

She's not a bit afraid, this genteel woman of Muusha, and it isn't because of false optimism or of a failure to realize the hellishness of her situation. She has no fear because fear, like food, like water, like even the seed once guarded for spring, is already long used up. Fear is a memory of better times. Fear is a dream. Perhaps fear will come back someday, along with the rain.

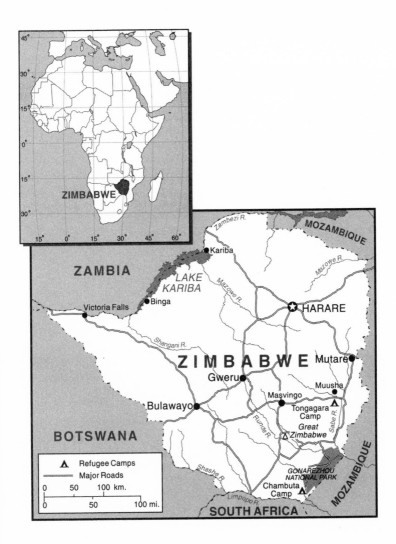

Those readers who would like to learn more about Save the Children or make a tax-deductible donation may write to:

Save the Children
54 Wilton Road
Westport, CT 06881
(203) 221-4000

MICHAEL DORRIS is the prize-winning author of numerous essays, short stories and many books, including *Morning Girl* (Hyperion Books, 1992), a young adult novel that both *Booklist* and *The New York Times Book Review* named a "Notable Book of 1992" and that won the Scott O'Dell Prize for historical fiction; *The Crown of Columbus* (HarperCollins, 1991), coauthored with Louise Erdrich, an international best-seller; *The Broken Cord* (Harper & Row, 1989), winner of the 1989 National Book Critics Circle award for nonfiction and *New York Times* best-seller; and a critically acclaimed novel, *A Yellow Raft in Blue Water* (Henry Holt, 1987). His books have been translated into fourteen languages.

Mr. Dorris won the 1992 Center for Anthropology and Journalism Award for Excellence. He received a Citation of Excellence from the Overseas Press Club for one of the essays in *Rooms in the House of Stone* (the essay was originally published in *Mother Jones* magazine). He holds an M.Phil. in anthropology from Yale and serves as adjunct professor in Native American Studies at Dartmouth College. He is married to the poet and novelist Louise Erdrich.

More from the Milkweed Editions Thistle series:

Bad Government and Silly Literature

Carol Bly

I Won't Learn from You!
The Role of Assent in Learning

Herbert Kohl

A Male Grief
Notes on Pornography and Addiction

David Mura

The Mythic Family

Judith Guest

MISSION STATEMENT

Milkweed Editions publishes with the intention of making a humane impact on society, in the belief that literature is a transformative art uniquely able to convey the essential experiences of the human heart and spirit.

To that end, Milkweed Editions publishes distinctive voices of literary merit in handsomely designed, visually dynamic books, exploring the ethical, cultural, and esthetic issues which free societies need continually to address. Milkweed Editions is a national not-for-profit press with a strong regional base.